ANOTHER LANGUAGE

ANOTHER
LANGUAGE

Poetry by Sue Saniel Elkind
Photography by Lori Burkhalter-Lackey

Papier-Mache Press
Watsonville, California

First Edition
96 95 94 93 92 10 9 8 7 6 5 4 3 2

ISBN: 0-918949-05-X

Printed in the United States of America.

Cover art by Deidre Scherer (Frieda, fabric and thread).

Copy editing by Bobbie Goodwin.

Thanks and acknowledgement to the following magazines for original publication of works included in this collection: *The Big Scream, Black Bear Review, Bottomfish, Brooklyn Review, Calyx, The Centennial Review, The Creative Woman, Crosscurrents, The DeKalb Literary Arts Journal, Iowa Woman, Kalliope, Kansas Quarterly, The Kindred Spirit, The Old Red Kimono, The Panhandler, Pig in a Poke, Pinchpenny, Pivot, Red Cedar Review, Riverrun, San Fernando Poetry Journal, Saxifrage, Thirteen, Windfall, Yellow Butterfly.*

Some poems were previously published in the following collections by Sue Saniel Elkind: *No Longer Afraid* (Lintel, 1985), *Waiting for Order* (Naked Man Press, 1988), and *Dinosaurs and Grandparents* (MAF Press, 1988). "Ashes in the Adirondacks" was selected for the 1986-87 *Anthology of Magazine Verse and Yearbook of American Poetry.*

Library of Congress Cataloging-in-Publication Data

Elkind, Sue Saniel, 1913-
    Another language : poetry / by Sue Saniel Elkind ;
photographs by Lori Burkhalter-Lackey.
      p. cm.
    ISBN 0-918949-05-X : $8.00
    1. Aging—Poetry. 2. Aged women—Poetry. I. Title.
PS35555.L475A56 1992
811'.54—dc20   92-20102
                                                               CIP

To my husband Will and my three grandchildren

Sue Saniel Elkind

Contents

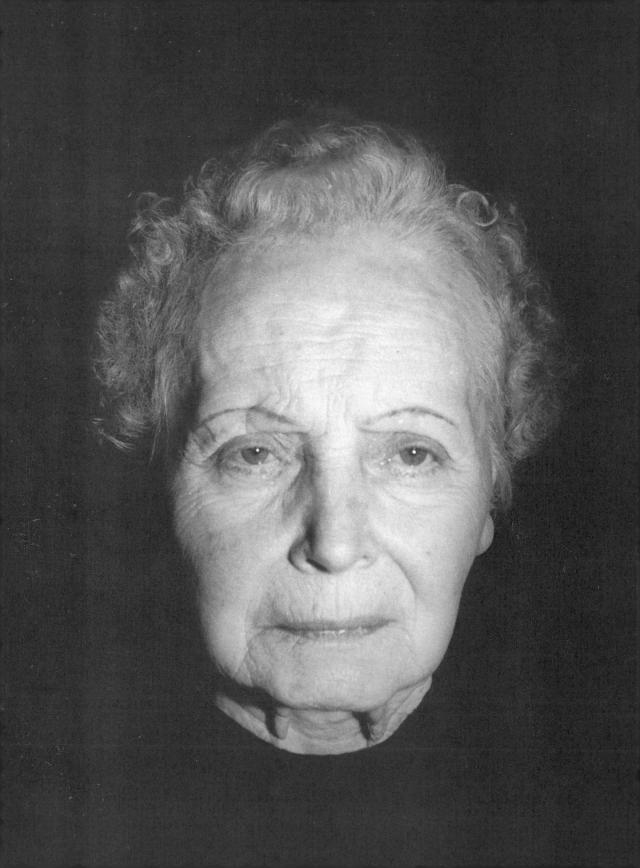

I Am

a reflection in a glass
a blur of a woman unable to see.
I am the sunset bleeding its pool
on the wall.
I am a chipped vessel
a dried reservoir
walls sagging,
a graveyard of stillborns,
an older version of a young woman
who calls me mother.
I am a sage with all the right answers
a verdant field crying for lovers,
an old lady who wants the comfort
of her mother's arms,
and I am the little child curled tight
hiding in the night
hiding the wrinkled face
of an old lady
wrinkled like a newborn.

Sharing

I sit with a young woman
whose age is half mine.
We share tea, biscuits,
and our sons so that
each may know her own son more.
Times anger boils like a kettle,
other times our pride
like freshly polished silver
shines on our faces.

Though it gets dark early
this time of year,
and I get old faster,
her voice soft, soothing,
helps me remember, warms
as the tea warms us.

We speak in that universal mother tongue
of school dances and feared wars,
of our sons, each so much his own man
yet so much still a part of us.

Forward

Mothers grow tired
in kitchens waiting, hoping
half their lives
for the son, the daughter
to carry a family
forward.

Today I'm flying
inside my own body
my heart beating
with pure joy and helium.
Even the wind can't reach me
as I soar, meet the sun
that huge gleaming jewel.
I'm rich
beyond all expectation
knowing both daughter
and son's wife will
carry this family
forward
'til these women, too, will stand
waiting, hoping.

To That Wall

This morning I put bread
in the toaster
sit silent as it burns

I'm moving across the world
to that thick wall
where letters to God
are stuffed in the cracks,
where I stuff my letter of joy,
ask that my daughters
be delivered of healthy babies,
where unformed words cry
in my throat knowing
I will not see
those babies

and the smoke rises
like clouds rising
above the mountains

The Night Grandfather Died

You were twice a child
the one in tears
and wheedlings first.
I watched you change
to infancy
then return to the crib
where one night I closed
your baby ancient eyes
and you became a man.

Eternal War

Amid the strife in this room
the only sound I hear
is the noise in my head—
machine of my anger—
that won't shut off.
Her words crank it keep it going.
I try to brake my body
keep from striking back know
we're on a collision course.
One of us will have to give but

I see only my mother
who hears no sounds yet knows well
the red anger of her child
who uses fists for words.
I am that child.

Now it is my daughter hurling words;
my daughter who blossomed each month
like the roses in the garden,
who seamed my belly
with its striae whose own belly
distended will soon wear
its stripes of sisterhood.

A Child Waiting

I wanted the past to go away
to leave it as I would my house,
shutting the door on it.

I wanted the past to go away   now
it's tomorrow, the future, whatever,
and my life has exploded,
shards flying through the air.

I see my daughter emptied
of the life she carried
so briefly,
my other daughter fighting
to hold on to the life in her womb
struggling against those tight quarters.

I wanted the past to go away,
shutting out the sounds of children
blending with wind chimes,
young bodies crashing into each other
like water against rocks,
to get the phone, the door.

Now I'm living in that past
every word is another daub on the palette
for the picture painted in memories.
I keep going backward until I know
I'll end up a child waiting
for a life of tomorrows.

Shivah

This week we don't ring
just walk into the house.
She sits covered in black
unshod on a crate
at the window
in a room
where all mirrors are draped
where a heavy candle burns
where nine men sway
beating their chests.
She is a dark stone
Her eyes dry now
Knuckles on balled hands
unclinch as she shakes a fist
berating God
for taking her son from her
taking from him
the pleasure
of seeing his children grow
for creating sunsets that bleed
into a house black
in its grief.

Self-Portrait

I listen to her
voice a knife cutting
as she carps at her husband.
Her child comes to her for a kiss
gets instead a look that gels
the blood.

I am what she will become,
face a map of years,
bulges where a waistline was,
thighs that were lean inviting.
How lithe she is,
how seductively she walks.
How I hate this woman
who is everything
I once was.

Grandmother's Hands

In the cracked winter morning
my hands rim the edge of the plate.
Numb from cold they become purple then
redden as the dawn sky turns red.

When did this happen
my hands becoming yours, grandmother?

invitation

when i received the letter inviting me
i was flattered   excited   then i wanted out
& didn't know how   now the day is here & i think
what am i doing in this place   keynote speaker
i'm no speaker much less capable of delivering
a keynote speech but here i am & there are all those eyes
peering at me studying me & yes evaluating me & me
i'm sizing them all up thinking god how old   i am
speaking to a roomful of dinosaurs   old   old   old
everyone in the room except me, of course, reeks of it
cries of it   when i begin a metamorphosis occurs
as years fall from faces like calendar leaves   while i
an old lady am speaking to a roomful of young   eager
vital people   boy i think i'd better be on my toes because
i can almost hear their minds computing   see questions
forming on lips & suddenly this is a challenge
to hell with my prepared speech this is going to be
a rap session   i'll say a few words off the cuff
& we'll talk & boy did i get put through the paces
mine was the mind that had to work fast or i'd lose them
but i tell you i've never had so much fun in my life
& when i get home i'll put a sign in my window
speaker available   call me

The Group

Why do we do this
every month
year after year
brush cheeks   kiss air
unzip our incisions
spill our guts   then
become kids
in grade school teasing
about things we did.

The time in eighth grade
I wore mother's silk stockings,
lipstick, and enough powder
for a line of chorus girls,

high school   our first dates—
how sophisticated we were!
How fast we ran!

Now in our mid-seventies
hiding from the fact
that once there were eight
now there are four.
Thinking, but never uttering
the one thought uppermost in our minds...

old lady & the station wagon

the other day i was walking home
a big station wagon was parked
in a driveway half in half out
i waited for the driver to go
he wouldnt & i coudnt   he was
too far out in the street too far back
in the drive the wagon was that long
finally i asked him nicely mind you
if he'd pull back just a bit and i could go on
but he was talking to some girls didnt hear
me i asked again feeling like a bad child
interrupting   smiled instead he backed up
i walked on the girls calling motherfucker
after me i heard a car speed up the street
pull into a driveway just as i got near
it was the same wagon the girls were in it now
yelling more obscenities that stung like hornets
the driver pulled out i walked on   again
this happened & i crossed the street
they pulled into each drive
on that side too the girls yelling
motherfuckercocksuckingbitch then
my legs soft putty   face livid
teeth clenched jaws aching
i took my house key & scratched the wagon
the man got out pushed me around took my wallet

because of the noise somebody called the police
there were no witnesses i was an old lady
with 5 young people calling me liar i hope
the street cleaners come tomorrow

Stalker

In clothing dark
as night,
the old lady walks
clutching groceries
in a sack.
She walks past
the restaurant,
the movie house,
the church,
to the bus stop,
her tongue pushing
her dentures in   out
left   right
never once missing the beat
never hearing
the other black figure
rhythm matching hers,
arms extended,
closing in
for the grab.

Night Scene

Head bent
against the rain and wind
buffeting his body
the old man didn't notice
the bright unwavering
stare of those eyes
coming closer
until they collided
body against body
knocking down the old man
leaving him, an emptied coat,
submerged in a puddle
waiting to be claimed.

HUD Section 231/8:
Federal Housing for the Elderly

The lobby shines,
smells from disinfectant,
empty of life, a desert.

I am taken to a room to observe
"a chorale of our darlings,
aren't they wonderful?"
Mouths move up and down
as Nancy Do-Gooder pulls
their strings and conducts.
I can't hear what they are singing;
they seem not to care about the song.

On my way out of the building
I see a woman take her father in,
hear her say, "You'll love it here,
Dad, with your own kind."
His eyes are flat and dry—
looking into the desert.

Camps

I.

Smiles
of false cheer mingle
with the acid stench
of senility
and the sounds
of endless, aimless shufflings
in this desert.

II.

Lost in a miasma
of age
I sit
in this one-room place.
I'd been told
I would like it.
I had not been told
people die here of loneliness.

III.

My dream bores
into bone marrow:
shattered glass
stained with blood
bits of flesh hanging
on barbed wire
shaved heads
numbers and smoke
stacks vomiting
numbers.

Heavy Baggage

Wave upon wave of light
filters through
the venetian blinds
yet the room is full
of my own dark.

I'm tired of carrying
the heavy baggage of my flesh:
brittle, numb,
but I'm afraid of letting go.

If I stop
I may be alone
unburied
in an open ditch
rotting
in smoke-sour air
like those in the camps.

Either way
I lose.

Old Man Sitting

The bones are brittle
as are the thoughts
they crumble
events of yesterdays that never happened
things that happened not remembered
today becomes another time
faces and events mingle
become a crazy quilt.

He sits and stares
unaware of a spreading map
in his crotch that moves down
his legs and becomes a puddle
at his feet.

His hands dangle at his sides
veiny gnarled
twitching
are they waiting for some message
from that dead brain
his pulse is almost an insult.

They say he feels no pain.

Way-Station

What made me think of her today?
Was it the music, the dancing;
she with her plastic hip,
she just learning to use a walker,
each step a journey.

There's no one who cares enough
to visit with her, only those who
share the narrow hallway,
from whose rooms cries blend with hers
becoming one long wail.

The lives of the old are
so delicately stitched
with their fine layers of muscle,
tissue, skin; one snip
and they unravel.

forgotten woman

she lies in a stelazine stupor
a skeleton
still
not enough bones
to count her years on
red specks move
on her bed
an army
surrounding her
leaving their wounds
a kind of covering
for her pleated skin
she lies there
unclaimed
by family
friends
death

Crossing the Street

An old man
thin ends of his beard
threads in the breeze
totters on his fragile frame
leans against a wall
gathering strength
for the journey.

First Rays

The gunmetal shadows of night
thin
and the first rays of dawn
unveil
a cosmetic dusting of white
on the rooftop and crocuses.

An old man sits at the table
his palsied hands
unable
to get food to his mouth.

Dark clouds hover,
mourners who wait for a call
that comes
when the old man gives up
and ground is broken.

Old Woman

Her hair, pale and wispy,
reminds me of the moon
behind the elm.
Her toothless lisp rises
to a raspy squeak
as she tells me
there are children
in the basement.
Their cries, laughter
distract. She says
she even hears her own voice
among the children,
is afraid to open the door,
afraid of what she'll find.

Her eyes are fireflies
as she talks, flashing brighter
with each word, then glazing over
as she stops mid-sentence,
nods off, then rouses herself,
walks to the door, listens,
hears only silence.
Eyes sparkling again she wants to know
where the children went.
She has milk and cookies for them.
She can't wait. She starts to eat.

Don't Be Afraid to Break
Bad News to the Aged

Her spine curves away
from the chair back
a perfect picture
of osteoporosis.
I'm afraid for her
now that I've said
her last friend's been placed
in a home.
She contemplates first
one hand then the other
as she rocks
'til I think I can't
bear the silence longer.
Then slowly she hoists
herself from the chair
says, "life sucks"
takes her cane
and walks.

Ashes in the Adirondacks

Mist rises up the sides
of the mountains like breath
in cold weather.

The landscape arranges itself,
pictures in an album
that turn brown in my hands.

Picking up some earth, I watch
it make furrows
on my fingers.

I shiver as I open the box
I carried here
to scatter my brother's remains
to the mountains, the wind.

My task completed, I become the last
of the family   and
leave as the last trace of mist
disappears.

On Being Seventy-Five

My mind's a freeway
of fractured thoughts
careening into each other.

I forget keys   names
even my own; wonder times
why I'm doing what I'm doing.

The dark comes sooner than expected.
I forget what I say soon
as the words are out, like:

"I don't want to get old
in traffic; please hold my hand."

My thoughts keep going like cars
in the wrong direction
on a one-way street   and

I hope my end will be as sudden
as the statistic that reads:
"Killed on impact."

Night Watch

Alone
on my bed, I listen
to the downpour as it smacks
the patio below.
I hear the wind
fling sheets
across the shingles of the house.
The yellow glow of gas lamps
on the street throws a pattern
on the wall of branches
switching madly in the wind.
Out through parted curtains
toward the city
the glimmering torrents slant down
in and out of the flicker
and the city slithers through
the blackness glistening
in the wet, its multicolored
scaly back catching sparks of neon.

I am afraid of the wind, heavy rains.
This will not be a night for sleeping.

old woman's pride

I fought the battle
lost it
when i picked up the phone
askcd
come stay with me
nights i'm afraid
alone

In a Fog
(Before cataract surgery)

Floundering frightened
I want my mother.
I look around for some sign
anything familiar
to give me a bearing.
Can't see street names
nor house numbers.
I slide on icy steps
steep as ski slopes.
Knock on doors ask for help,
voices speak to me—
when they speak—
through solid oak.
I feel like Alice
growing smaller
'til I'm a baby wrinkled
wearing old ladies' clothes
crying tears
that freeze on wizened cheeks.

Prologue

Am I dying here in this strange room,
life seeping slowly out with each breath?
Faces are suspended over me,
someone prays over me—
I who never prayed at all.
Is this a prologue to death?

Nurses come and go with little trays
hiding needles under layers of white.
Everything around me is white—
shining bright white, until I close my eyes
and there's an explosion of red:
red the color of blood, of anger,
of birth, of hell.

My daughter looks down at me.
I see myself in her pitying eyes,
know I'm getting ugly   dressed
in age's leathery skin.
I try to think back to what it was like
in the beginning,   but

I have been jabbed three times tonight,
fallen into a surf of red, and now I am alone,
unguarded, as I enter my own deepening dusk.

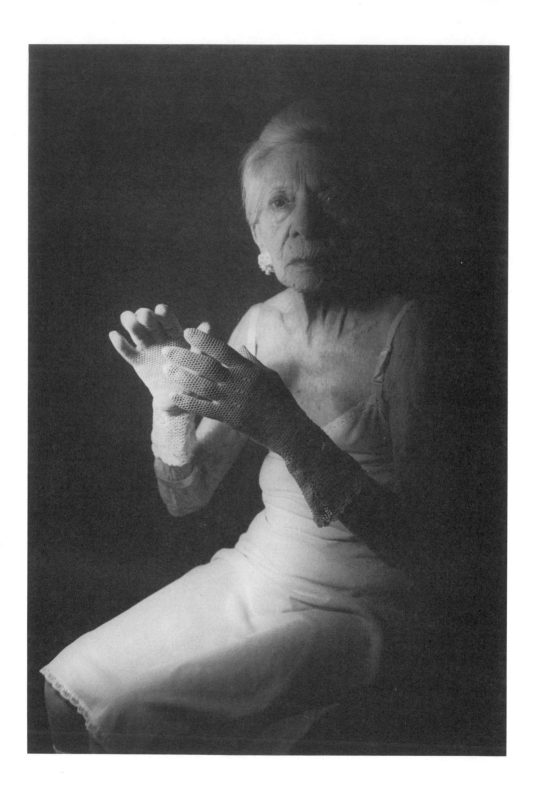

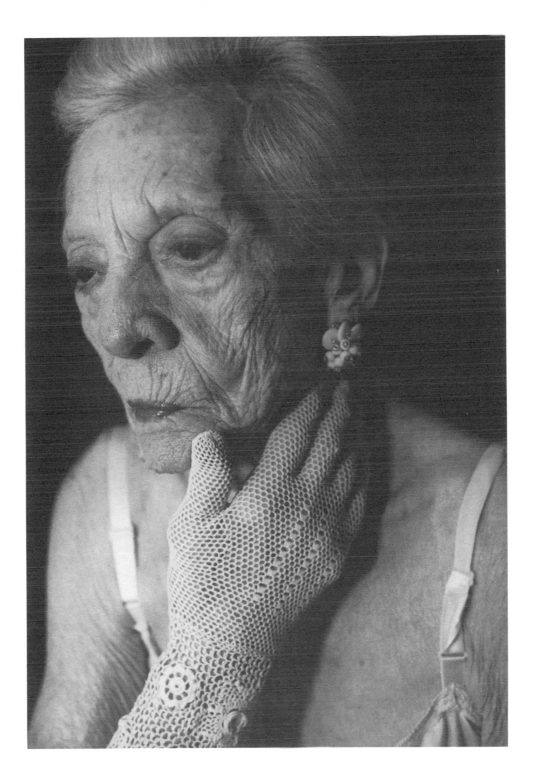

Another Language

It's beginning   and
I'm frightened.

Fruit rots,
leaves curl
into their stems.

Already the stink of my own
body fluids permeates.
My skin pulls away
from dried bones.
Through sparse hair
my skull shines white.

My daughter speaks
a language I don't understand.
My words stop mid-sentence   yet
I recite the names of ancestors.

I'd like to pull in
the chains of my eyes
see that blessed black   but
yesterdays become tomorrows,
tomorrows become years.
Everyone grows younger.

Silent Cry

One of the horrors of old age
visited me yesterday when
I sat talking with my son
and couldn't remember
his wife's name.
He stared at me, I stared
into space wanting to sweep
the corners
hoping her name would drop
from between my lips. Frightened
I wondered is this what IT is like?
Has IT finally happened to me?
Will I be encased in this membrane
waiting for the blood to hit my brain?
I'm too young, I'm only seventy-five,
this never happened to my parents.
It was much better when everyone I'd meet
would remind me of someone else I'd met
when each person was a patchwork quilt
with pieces of others stitched
here and there, the voice reminds me of—
the smile reminds me of—the shape
of the head—the walk.
Were we neighbors once, did we go to school
together, did you once ask me to dance
at the prom, who are you anyway?
I don't remember your name.

Old Child

Old, I think like a child
one minute
an adult the next:
a young girl smiling
coyly, flirting,
an old lady forgetting
the empty spaces in her mouth.

I'm death waiting,
a bride shyly unbuttoning
her dress
for a husband
a memory
nightly
in her room.

Senility

It happens
suddenly
One day
you open your mouth
and sounds
come out like scrabble tiles
when all you pick
are consonants.

Reflections

I listen to the music   when
I see them   young   holding each other
close as they dance   each movement
a melody until the music stops
they stroll out   touching only
by the look between them
I turn away   see reflected
in the mirror opposite me
an old woman   staring   how dare she
intrude on this moment   I reach
for an ash tray   hurl it at the mirror
then covering my face with my hands
feel it shatter

Grass

Grass comes apart
when I lie down on it.
Separate and flat.

Youth is separate,
lives unto itself.
No need to glance

in a mirror,
see the damage done
by that surgeon of years,

see hanging flesh,
scar tissue of time,
creasing in places
that once shined like grass.

Dinosaurs and Grandparents

"...as old as you, Grandma?"
when I take my grandson to the museum.

How old I must seem to him.
I think: if I put my foot over
the dinosaur's I'd move
in the same direction.

What do children know about pain
in the bones of the old,
or how far they risk walking alone?
When my husband and I walk
so close together even the wind can't
get in, it's because we feel everything
under us moving.

In the silence of the night
I hear the earth turn.
It's then I make the connection.

Grandson

You are
a porcelain figurine
If I touch your fingers
they might snap
You gaze back at me
as if you know
what I'm feeling
Your hand grasps my finger
and for a moment
it's I who'll come apart.
I rock you
back and forth
still you stare into my eyes
as if reading me
then with the wisdom
of your few weeks
you close your eyes
not to see my tears
as I rock
and hold your mother
once again in my arms.

Granddaughter

Loving transfigures.

My face changes
when my granddaughter
looks at me
and it becomes real
as loneliness
or birds singing.

In Praise of Peepholes

Hearing them stamp
the snow off their feet
I look through the peephole
even before the bell rings.
I did not invite them,
know if I let them in
they'll say
they can't stay
but will.
Inside, they'd discover:
me at age seventy
my teeth out of place
in a glass on the table,
the boxes full of poems,
my collection of magazines
and other litter.
If I let them
into my swelling house,
my dwindling life,
they will only add to the mess
with their soiled wet shoes,
make a scene
at my not having told them
it's my birthday.
Praise be the peephole.
I don't have to
let them in.

After Forty-Five Years of Marriage

Fifteen thousand nine hundred twenty days
of marriage (not counting leap years)
Forty-seven thousand seven hundred sixty
meals prepared (not counting snacks)
thirty-one thousand eight hundred forty times
sweeping the kitchen floor
Three thousand ties received for Xmas gifts
returned for him
Some nine hundred fifty-four thousand
two hundred diapers changed, an equal number
of bottoms cleaned and powdered
Fifty pairs of slacks ironed
with knife-like creases on the sides
until he patiently mentioned "Men's slacks
have the crease down the front."
Too many hundreds of socks darned to hear
"Sue, you made the socks too small again."
Dishes washed: millions; but why go on counting.
Now we celebrate our 45th anniversary
and I have a burning hope we'll receive
no gifts I've no space for any more
"what is its" and if I handle another glass
or plate it'll simply slide through my fingers
then I'll have yet another time to sweep
the kitchen floor.

Shells

Together in
the same house
the same bed
Two snails
curling inward
inward until
nothing but
two shells each
in their places
growing old
separately.

Holding On

We came together
fifty years ago
strangers who look alike
have assumed each other's mannerisms.
Words are scarce between us.
Two unmendable old things
sharing the same bed
the same plate
the same corner,
skeletal,
we hold on to each other
afraid of what might happen
if one let go.

Time for Muted Lights

When the plastic kitchen chairs
begin to crack
and the fabric on the footstool
shows its stuffing,
when the sink begins to list
like a sinking boat

pulling away from its mooring,
when the breasts begin to go
and the skin under your chin hangs loose
and in the mirror you see
the wrinkles around the eyes

grow and deepen
when you feel like an aged courtesan
undressing in front of him

you know it's time for muted lights
in the collapsing house of your life.

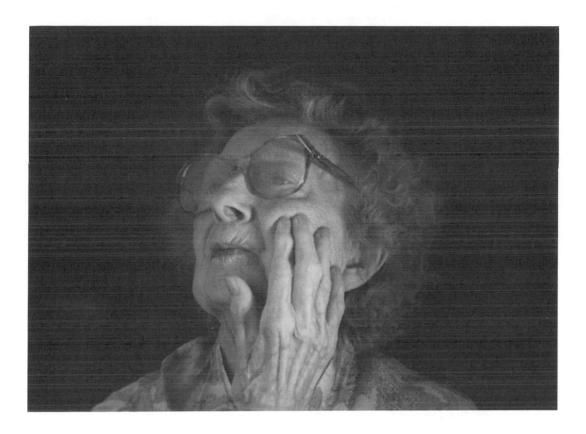

Is It Because I'm Old?

Why can't you look at me
in the daylight
or at night when
the lights are on
or take my hand
as you once did
and press it to your mouth?
Is it because I'm no longer
beautiful that I'm old?

If only you'd shovel
back the dark and speak.

A New Creation

At night
we go down a long slide
into a secret chamber.

We have tickets for this ride
but can't find ourselves
in the trick mirrors.

We lie down in fetal position
snails back to back
eyes open   waiting.

Even though we've shared
this space fifty years
there's always that dread

until sunrise
another creation
another miracle

when all the fears of the night
turn into leaves on limbs
of trees and (for awhile)
we're safe again.

Come to Me

Come to me looking
as you did fifty years ago
arms outstretched
and I will be waiting
virgin again
in white that changes
to splashes of roses
as we lie together.
Come to me smiling again
with your mortar and pestle
and vitamin pills
because I am given to colds
and coughs that wrack us both.
Oh! come to me again
and I will be there
waiting with withered hands
gnarled fingers
that will leave their marks
of passion on your back.

The Last

I look up
past the sun
deep into the window of the sky
into the universe

I am the last of winter
losing my tenuous hold
falling
into an eddy whirling
alone I find myself
in a place I've never been

The root of heaven
or the lid of hell
It must be purgatory
a place of decision
of waiting

Someone stops
tramples me
I lie still at last
a leaf fallen

Before Rosh Hashanah

is the time
of remembrance
to visit the graves
of loved ones
say prayers for their souls.

An aged couple
kneels over the grave
of their son.
In that cold tunnel
his skin has already fallen off
his bones dried   white.

I hear their sobs
see on their bent heads
where their skulls are already visible   and

I remember other days
bare branches whipping
when my parents visited their son's grave
how they, too, sobbed.

I go over to the couple
pray for them   their boy
unaware that my own skull
already shines white in the sun.

Alone at Eighty-Four

She roams her empty house,
an abandoned child   hoping
to be found

She pulls the drapes   longing
for a face to bleed in

She climbs
into the lives of strangers
sets her heart by their time

When I call
her words   hang
in the air
in search of a sentence

When I hang up
I cry   knowing
she is a death   waiting
to be eulogized

Sisters

We exhumed ghosts
of our childhood
exorcised them
along with past angers
then laughed
at family legends as we
laid to rest old antagonisms
She was no longer a threat
her beauty lost somewhere
in the two years
since we'd been together
She eighty-two
face a map
of many roads traveled
body bent withered
a dying tree
I seventy-two already
felt the imminent loss
of a sister
finally accepted
who brought me African violets
to remember
she remembered
I always loved them

Detour

Even with death approaching
she is demanding:
"call this one, call that one,
tell them all to get right over,
tomorrow will be too late."
They all come—twelve
and a nurse to round it out
as they make a circle around her bed—
a perfect coven of crows.

They advance, retreat,
their soft sides pulsing
in, out, wing-wide, never touching
humming their hums,
crooning their mystical liturgy
then

she stands
tall on her bed,
hair a bird's nest in its disorder,
hospital gown a-flap, exposing
that age tired body,
orders them: "be still,
I want to sleep now."

Once again death is detoured.

Ethel
(1903-1988)

I.

I want to scream my frustration
and anger. Two months she's been
in that hospital, two months of daily
phone calls, two months of hating
my own immobility, of wondering what
her doctor doesn't tell me,
and there's nothing, *nothing* I can do!
Just keep calling and listening
to the ravings one day, the seeming calm
the next that lulls me into a false upswing.
I want to rock her, cradle her
but the closest I can get
is the telephone, so I cradle it
like a baby or an old lady.

II.

First it was her wheelchair
taken from her room, then
it was "the walker I got
twenty-seven years ago
that had my name engraved on it."
My knuckles are white as I clench
the receiver in one hand, tear
at the buttons on my dress
with the other.
This isn't the sister I cared for,
fought with, whose beauty I envied—
this poor, toothless old lady.

III.

"Listen, they're playing the Minute Waltz.
Do you remember when I used to play that,
how Mama loved it? I'll have to play it
for her when I get better. She'll wait
by the window, watch for Papa to come home,
hum along, but you don't believe me, do you?"
How can I tell her our parents have been dead
almost thirty years.

Then there's a silence—a dead phone—
death   death   death
until her nurse says to me,
"Ethel's too tired for more words."
When I put down the phone my hand is full
of buttons, my dress, open, exposes
my grief and anger.

IV.

Already I hear them
shoveling the earth
for her grave.

Final Breaths

The evening sun
falls through the window
covering her,
sliding down her arms
onto the floor,
a blazing river

spilling inside her room.
I see her in the light
wearing her skeleton tied tight
and smooth over her belly.

I don't touch her,
just watch her chest
rise and fall with labored breaths
glad she is still alive
as I stumble to her,

smooth her with promises
smell the milky wrinkle of her skin
and grasp the small shape of her life
tight in my arms.

Moment of Truth

The trees know
in their winter barrenness.
I know from a voice
coming through cables,
snakes
coiling   uncoiling
underground,
miles and miles of them
that finally reach their prey.
And what could I do?
It's done.
She's all used up now;
dead as our brother is,
as our parents are.
I'm left at the end
of that line
alone as she
her lungs gagging,
heart straining
until God—in whom she had
no belief—
decides
it's time for her
to know.

I Will Say Kaddish for You, Sister

How can I think of you gone
when there was no one to mourn with
No one to see whether I sat shoeless
whether I sat on a wooden crate
whether I burned a candle for eight days
whether I beat my breast, wailed my grief
in proper Jewish fashion
when there is no one to share your life with.

How can I think of you gone
if I wasn't there?
All I could touch was a telephone
through which I listened to your
pneumonic cough, not even able to hold
a sputum tray for you when you were too weak
Not there to fight for the dignity torn
from you by nurses who so easily unbound
your suffering body from a lucid mind
Not there to cover you when you were left bare
on your bed for all to see how age shriveled,
how your breasts lay flaccid, empty sacks
with their brown nipples—obscene adornments.

Not there to soothe when confusion set in
and innocent teenagers turned into Nazis
coming after you and all Jews
Not there to see you hide your numbers

to offer reassurances that you were safe
Not there to hold your hand
escort you from this life to that other—
to kiss you one last time.

I will say Kaddish for you, sister,
though I may mispronounce the words,
because I know how much that prayer meant to you.
I will say it alone.

Scattered Ashes

We walk close, my husband and I,
as we climb this hill to the cemetery.
I feel as if we're walking over
the earth's rim and will disappear.

The promise to my sister is heavy
in my hands.
I want to say to my husband,
"Where are our children,
we need them close now,"

but they are scattered
as these ashes will be.
We touch shoulders
to hold ourselves together.

After Rosh Hashanah

The apples have turned
brown on the dish.
The honey filmed over
in the pot.

Here I am in the kitchen
again not knowing why.
There's nothing to prepare for
but I look for something to do.
In this room that has always been
a sanctuary to me,
I find no comfort today.

Fold a sheet of paper
and the ink repeats.
How can I make time repeat?
We forgot to take pictures.

I go into the rooms they've left,
see the umbrella, my grandson's toy,
and I remember my mother saying
"If guests forget something
it means they'll be back."

Out the window I see
a family of hummingbirds
hover over the flowers
then scatter.

From a distance
I hear the ram's horn.

This Year/Next Year

As always at this time of year
I call the roll:
my parents, sister, brother;
just one old aunt is left,
her head almost bald.
Year after year at the Seder table
she still leans to the side.

Her gnarled fingers flounder
at her breasts twisting
the dial as she turns up
her hearing aid.
Still I shout at her,
angry at her age,
angry at Elija's untouched cup,
angry at those missing,
but most of all angry
at hearing the old aunt say:
"Next year in Jerusalem"
when I know she'll never get there.

Legacy

In this my final season
I try to justify my existence.
As winter empties itself of color,
as the birds leave,
as the sun pales,
I rebel.

Next door my neighbor feeds
his bonfire with the last
raked leaves   while
I feed my freezer
with new recipes.

I used to want peace,
a place to hide
to be lost in.
Now I have the place,
if being alone is being lost
and silence is peace.

Sue Saniel Elkind

Sue Saniel Elkind was born in 1913 in Pittsburgh, Pennsylvania, where she has remained all of her life. After attending the University of Pittsburgh for one year, she quit school to work in an insurance office. She married William Elkind in 1940 and has a son, James Saniel Elkind, a daughter, Carol Elkind Poll, and three grandchildren.

Local community service has played a large role in Ms. Elkind's life. She helped organize a seniors program at the Pittsburgh Jewish Community Center. Later, she established and operated a foster home placement program through Craig HouseTechnoma, a day school and hospital for emotionally disturbed children and teenagers.

She began writing poetry at the age of sixty-four. Recognizing the need to interact with other writers, she founded the Squirrel Hill Poetry Workshop under the sponsorship of the Carnegie Library. Well known in the Pittsburgh area, the group published its first anthology in 1990. A second anthology is forthcoming.

Ms. Elkind has four other collections of poetry: *Bare As the Trees* (Papier-Mache Press, 1992), *Waiting for Order* (Naked Man Press, 1988), *Dinosaurs and Grandparents* (MAF Press, 1988), and *No Longer Afraid* (Lintel, 1985). Her work has appeared in over 150 magazines and reviews. She was a recipient of the 1987 Esther Scheffler Poetry Award of Michigan State University.

Lori Burkhalter-Lackey

Lori Burkhalter-Lackey was born and educated in Los Angeles, completing her photographic training at Otis/Parsons Art Institute. Her work has been exhibited in many California galleries, and she recently completed several documentary photographic assignments in Paris.

In 1987 her photographs were featured prominently in the Papier-Mache Press anthology about women and aging, *When I Am an Old Woman I Shall Wear Purple*. In this latest collection Lori attempts to capture the wisdom and dignity of an aging America.

She would like to give special thanks to the Sepulveda Convalescent Hospital of Los Angeles for giving her the opportunity to know, love, and photograph its residents.

Lori currently lives in Los Angeles with her husband David and their three cats.

Deidre Scherer

Deidre Scherer is a visual artist who works in fabric and thread. She has focused on creating images of aging in a special series on death and dying, *The Last Year*.

A resident of Williamsville, Vermont, she received a Bachelor of Fine Arts from the Rhode Island School of Design. She was selected as an Artist-in-Residence by the Vermont Council of the Arts in 1978. Her long list of credits includes numerous group and solo exhibitions, and her work is often featured in magazines, including *Threads* (April 1988) and *Hospice* (Fall 1991).

Deidre Scherer's acclaimed fabric portraits of older women grace the covers of two other Papier-Mache Press anthologies: the award-winning bestseller, *When I Am an Old Woman I Shall Wear Purple*, and its companion, *If I Had My Life to Live Over I Would Pick More Daisies*.

Quality Books from Papier-Mache Press

At Papier-Mache Press our goal is to produce attractive, accessible books that deal with contemporary personal, social, and political issues. Our titles have found an enthusiastic audience in general interest, women's, new age, and Christian bookstores, as well as gift stores, mail order catalogs, and libraries. Many have also been used by teachers for women's studies, creative writing, and gerontology classes, and by therapists and family counselors to help clients explore personal issues such as aging and relationships.

If you are interested in finding out more about our other titles, ask your local bookstores which Papier-Mache items they carry. Or, if you would like to receive a complete catalog of books, posters, shirts, and postcards from Papier-Mache Press, please send a self-addressed stamped envelope to:

Papier-Mache Press
PO Box 1304
Freedom, CA 95019